Open Secret

Amanda Szulc

Presentation by *BookLeaf Publishing*

Web: www.bookleafpub.com

E-mail: info@bookleafpub.com

ISBN: 9789357696609

First edition 2023

DEDICATION

To my family: I will always be grateful for your support and your encouragement.

To the friends who stuck by me, even when I was wrong, you know who you are and I can't thank you enough.

To the people who wronged me, I bet you cursed the day you hurt me. You were warned.

ACKNOWLEDGEMENT

These poems are for the dreamers. To the ones who feel like their emotions and feelings are too big and so they feel the need to suppress them. You are not alone. You are worthy of everything beautiful this world has to offer.

PREFACE

This is a glimpse into moments in my life. Moments that defined me, broke me, made me stronger, and challenged me in so many ways. I hope that these words can heal you in some way.

These poems are either random thoughts that came to me, or they were inspired by someone. They are all original works and the feelings are authentic and true.

As someone who has 24 years of experience of playing piano and studying music, I have always been fascinated with the patterns of words and using them to express emotion. This book was a labor of love since I have hundreds of poems that I have written over the course of 17 years. Hopefully, this will be the first of many books so I continue to share my works with you.

City lights

Out of breath in a city full of fresh air
Choking on the tears I'm holding back
The last time I was here, you were mine
Another place and another time
How long will it take until I'm over you?

Realization

You got what you wanted
I thought that it was me
I was shiny and new
Too good for you
All the lies turned out to be true
Ridden with guilt
Written with tears
Your joy turned out to be my biggest fear
I'm left in the background in the story of your life

The wrong choice

I'll never be the one you choose
In this game we're playing I can't stand to lose
I sit her clutching my necklace like a life raft
Getting lost down my own path
Your jaded smile and your attitude
Makes me think that he owns you
I had him first, I claimed that man
But to you I'm just secondhand
I'll never be you
I sit here and think about the times you told me you
wanted me
You called me baby
Yet you never said you loved me
Every time she looks at you I pinch myself hard
To wake myself up from this nightmare
You're my rock star fantasy
You're unattainable yet you're right in front of me
I'm done feeling like trash
I deserve better than you

But at what cost?

I want to save you
But at what cost?
The cost of the pennies I threw into the fountain
Wishing for you to change your ways
The cost of the coins reflecting the sun on the
sidewalk
I took as a sign that my light would shine through
your darkness
The smoothness of the dollars I saved for us to get
away together
So much smoother than the course of life you took
without me
The jingling of the coins in my purse
Reminded me of the music you said we would make
together
As I write this poem by the river and as the wind
turns my silent tears cold
I spend my time like money
Praying you're safe

Healing

Sometimes the honest truth hurts worse than the
pretty lies
You're back to your old ways again
You have pushed me off the cliff where we once
watched the sun set
You cut me out of your life and the ties that bound
me to you fell to the ground
My heart is not a place for your brokenness
My tears are not a balm for your sadness
All the nights I laid awake were wasted time
Now I need to heal myself and take back whats mine

My mistake

I'm sorry
I'm sorry for trusting you
I'm sorry for saying "I love you" too quickly
I'm sorry for the way you let me open up to you
I'm sorry for the way you laughed at my jokes
I'm sorry for the way you would study my face when
I talked, making me blush
I'm sorry for the way we would listen to music
together on your couch with my head on your
shoulder, while the traffic passed by outside
I want to tell you how I feel, but I can't bring myself
to put together the words.
Now you have someone new
So all I can say is " I'm sorry"

Loaded gun

I have my questions ready like a loaded gun

Trying my best to laugh and say that this is fun

Let my feelings become numb

This is what I've become

As cold as the wind that blows outside my
bedroom window

As I talk to you

You are so kind

You open my eyes and I am blinded by your
light

But you must understand I'm not used to this

This unexpected bliss

Of finding someone who really cares

I will learn eventually to open up

But for now please go easy on me

I am learning

I am trying my best

To fight back my fears and make room for the
rest of the beautiful life that I see in your eyes

River tears

I sat by the river today and I thought of you

How the rushing of the water reminded me of your melodic laugh

How the small waves against the rocks mimicked the gentle way you used to caress my face

The cold water is completely opposite to your warm embrace

No matter what I do, I can't seem to forget you

You left a mark on me that will never fade

Like the cracks in the pavement along the riverbank

I wish I could just dive into the cleansing water and let it wash away all the memories I have of you

But for now, the reflections I see in the water are the last of us

They can float away forever.

Hotel Indigo

Meet me at the Hotel Indigo
Near the river walk where the cool waters flow
Let me lean my head on your shoulder
As we listen to the sound of the world turning over
Let's kiss underneath the covered bridge
Pick out a house where we might live
People say we move too fast
That what we have will never last
You say if they're right then who the hell cares
We love each other fearlessly with plenty left to spare
Whether we're near or far apart
Know that you will always have my heart

Sick obsession

You only care about me when you're drunk.
The liquor that you consume breaks down your walls.
Allows you to say things you've always held back
from me.
But when the morning light shines through your
window
You don't remember a thing
You laugh and pass off the night of your weakness
like it was a joke.
But you forget that it was me on the other end.
Me, who stayed up for hours to make sure you got
home safe.
Me, whose lines you fed and I ate them up like candy.
This is fine I say. At the moment it's all a game.
But I really don't want to play anymore

I didn't

I wanted to see you tonight
But I didn't
Instead I got drunk and listened to your favorite
songs
The ones that you said inspired you as a person
I wanted to call you and tell you how much I missed
you
But I didn't
Instead I stared at my phone as if I was staring into
your dark eyes
Something keeps holding me back
I want to tell you how I feel
Say everything that I never said
But I don't
And sadly, I never will

Dive Bar

Farthest seat in the back of the bar
Counting down the hours until I can go to my car
My hands are shaking as I sip my drink
A room full of strangers gives me time to think
How the hell did I get here
Where was my mind
As I put on my makeup and dressed up nice
I don't do this for just anyone but for you I did
I made the effort, withstood the pain
Got lost looking for the bar while driving in the
pouring rain
How could you treat me this way
After what you told me just the other day
Saying you wanted nothing more than to take me
home
So that I would feel less alone
Now all I want is the comfort of my home

Hickory House

Video games and magic shows in the basement
The indie music scene and jumping on trampolines
Countless family gatherings
It may seem like an ordinary house
But there is history here
It is sacred
Built by the hands of a man of God
If these walls could talk
They would speak of the laughter and chatter that
filled every room
If the floors could talk
They would speak of the many people that danced
and walked their way through here
Every room holds a memory for me
This entire house was the one thing that remained the
same no matter what changed in my life
I will treasure the memories forever

My prayer

There were times when I doubted the Lord's love for me. As the hardships came I cried out "God why have you forsaken me? Where are you as the world that I know, the world that I live in, is falling apart? I feel like I am losing everything that matters to me."

But then I caught a glimpse of your glory. I saw the pain you went through on Calvary.
Indeed, you loved me. You loved me through it all.
Through every trial, through every tear I cried, you were there.
You are with me now.
All those things I thought were SO important were mere fragments compared to your radiance. Mere fragments compared to your grace and your mercy.
So many times I have fallen short of your glory and your majesty.
So many times I have sinned in your eyes.
Loving myself more than others and most importantly, you oh Lord. These earthly pleasures are vain but now and forever I'll seek your name. I will forever love you.

Here I am oh Lord.
Your grace and mercy covers me.
Let me be surrounded by your love.
Your blood has paid the atonement for my sins.
In you I am a new creation.

In you I am forgiven. And I will dwell in Heaven
forever and ever.
Let your purifying fire seep through my heart into
my veins and let your love shine in my life.
All I am, all that I have let it be yours.
 I surrender my life to you.
I have stumbled so many times before. But you
always there.
I just needed to trust that you would catch me, draw
me gently to my knees and keep me near the cross.

I don't have to face this uncertain future alone. I have
you with me Lord. You know the plans.
Plans to give me a hopeful, bright future. I now know
for certain I will spend the rest of eternity with you.
And that life is worth living is you are living for the
Lord.

Help me forgive the ones who hurt me.
Let me give my pain, my sadness to you, and let me
be led by you into the future you have set before me.
Help forgive my enemies and do good to those who
reject me.

Thank you Lord, for giving me this life, so that I may
live for you and show your love to everyone around
me.

Amen.

Pain

A cage
A paralyzing fear with no explanation
A heavy weight on my chest
The racing thoughts
The scary thoughts
The nightmares
Questioning my faith
Questioning everything
Wondering why is God allowing this to happen to me
The days where I don't have the strength to leave my
bed
Trying to reach out for help but there is often no
answer
In a world gone mad I must try and stay sane
It is so hard
It's a daily battle
This is my anxiety and depression
So many metaphors yet unfortunately they are all true
I am trying my best to stay strong

Longing

I long to be happy again
I am grateful for what I have
But when I say I'm fine I don't mean it
My mind races and I can't relax
I don't sleep well
I'm trying my best
But I am lonely
I have so much love to give
Will things get better?
Will I be happy?
When will the questions be answered?

Little black dress

Little black dress
Hanging in the back of my closet
As I pick it off the hanger suddenly my mind is
flooded with memories
Diamond dust
Flashing neon lights
Spiked high heels
Beer bottles on the table
The sound of glasses coming together in celebration
Smiling with the microphone in my manicured hands
As the drums and guitar and bass blend together
As the crowd gathers on the dance floor
I see that this is the closest thing I have to a rock star
life
Memories more clear than any photograph
When I'm with this band I don't think about my
chronic pain
Or the stresses of everyday life
All the negativity fades away
Like dirt on the sidewalk after the rain
I'll treasure these moments forever

Ice in my heart

You are someone who I think about all year long.
Throughout the changing seasons.
But when the winter comes and the snow is falling
quietly on the ground, thats when your memory
consumes me.
On icy roads in my car when all I hear is my music.
The silence outside that pierces my heart.
The cold and unforgiving wind that shakes me.
As I sit alone sipping my wine, I'm reminded of who
I lost.
I hope and pray for things to be different when the
warmer weather comes.
For now, I will reminisce on better days.

Fourth of July

Another day that's come and passed
Another day that doesn't last
Another day without you near
Another day with thoughts of you, my dear
I'm sitting on the front porch step
Listening to the fireworks overhead
The night is so beautiful
Yet I just want to crawl into bed
My heart aches for you
As I watch the sun set fade
There's an emptiness inside me
That I can't explain
I hope that wherever you are, that you are safe
That you are well
With you I feel like heaven
Without you, I'm in hell

Gaslight

You don't love me anymore
It's taken me a while to realize it
But now that I know
I fully understand why you've been so distant
Why is it when I reminisce about the memories
we shared you are silent
You shut me down
Till I too, am scared into silence

Lake Life

Dandelion wishes
Butterfly kisses
The lake and the sweet summer air
Feeling the wind in my hair
I can't believe I'm here with you
We're holding hands along the canal
Getting ice cream at the parlor
It doesn't seem real
This feels like a scene from all the romance movies
and novels I grew up watching and reading
It's real and it's pure
Our love is forever
I know this to be true
It's in the way you look at me
You listen fully when I speak
The reassurance of your hand in mine as we walk
together
My family loves you
I see my future in your eyes
This road has not been easy to find each other
But we made it, my love
Our love is forever